A HEALTHY LIFE

Keeping Clean

by Kirsten Chang

BLASTOFF! READERS

BELLWETHER MEDIA · MINNEAPOLIS, MN

Blastoff! Readers are carefully developed by literacy experts to build reading stamina and move students toward fluency by combining standards-based content with developmentally appropriate text.

Level 1 provides the most support through repetition of high-frequency words, light text, predictable sentence patterns, and strong visual support.

Level 2 offers early readers a bit more challenge through varied sentences, increased text load, and text-supportive special features.

Level 3 advances early-fluent readers toward fluency through increased text load, less reliance on photos, advancing concepts, longer sentences, and more complex special features.

★ **Blastoff! Universe**

Reading Level

BLASTOFF! Beginners — Grade **K**

BLASTOFF! READERS — Grades **1–3**

BLASTOFF! DISCOVERY — Grade **4**

This edition first published in 2022 by Bellwether Media, Inc.

No part of this publication may be reproduced in whole or in part without written permission of the publisher. For information regarding permission, write to Bellwether Media, Inc., Attention: Permissions Department, 6012 Blue Circle Drive, Minnetonka, MN 55343.

Library of Congress Cataloging-in-Publication Data

Names: Chang, Kirsten, 1991- author.
Title: Keeping clean / Kirsten Chang.
Description: Minneapolis, MN : Bellwether Media, [2022] | Series: A healthy life | Includes bibliographical references and index. | Audience: Ages 5-8 | Audience: Grades K-1 | Summary: "Developed by literacy experts for students in kindergarten through grade three, this book introduces the importance of keeping clean to young readers through leveled text and related photos"–Provided by publisher.
Identifiers: LCCN 2021041254 (print) | LCCN 2021041255 (ebook) | ISBN 9781644875803 (library binding) | ISBN 9781648346651 (paperback) | ISBN 9781648345913 (ebook)
Subjects: LCSH: Hygiene–Juvenile literature. | Health–Juvenile literature.
Classification: LCC RA780 .C43 2022 (print) | LCC RA780 (ebook) | DDC 613–dc23
LC record available at https://lccn.loc.gov/2021041254
LC ebook record available at https://lccn.loc.gov/2021041255

Editor: Rebecca Sabelko   Designer: Andrea Schneider

Printed in the United States of America, North Mankato, MN.

Table of Contents

Squeaky Clean

Kate washes her hands. She uses soap and water. She dries off with a towel.

Why Is Keeping Clean Important?

Keeping clean
helps us stay healthy.

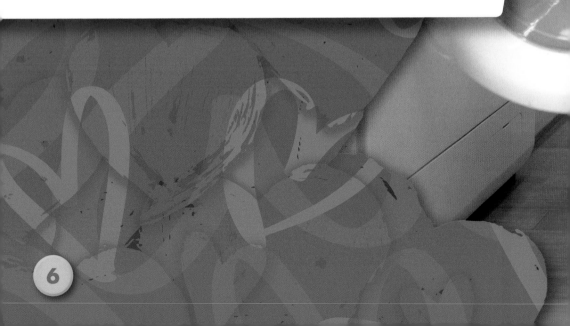

Germs can make us sick. Cleaning keeps germs away.

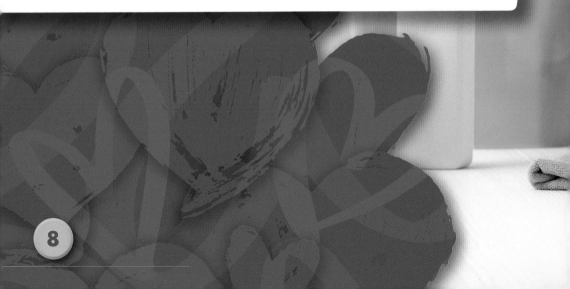

Being clean helps us feel more **confident**. We feel good about ourselves!

How Does Keeping Clean Help?

stay healthy

keeps germs away

feel confident

We might get sick if we do not clean ourselves. We could feel less confident.

How Do We Keep Clean?

Luke takes a bath. He washes his hair with **shampoo** and his body with soap.

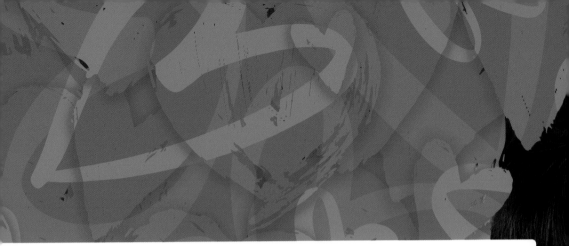

Gwen brushes
her teeth. Then she
uses **floss**. This keeps
her teeth strong.

flossing teeth

Tools for Keeping Clean

shampoo

soap

toothbrush, toothpaste, and floss

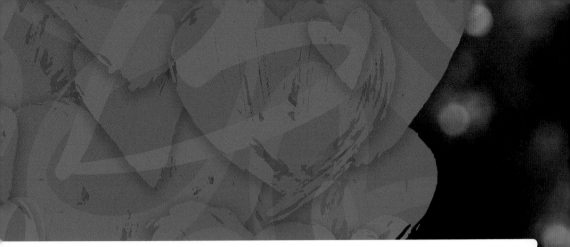

Achoo! Max covers
his mouth when
he sneezes. He keeps
others safe.

Luna loves to wear clean clothes. She feels ready for the day!

Glossary

confident

feeling good about yourself

germs

very small living things that can make you ill

floss

a type of thin thread used to clean between your teeth

shampoo

soap that is used to wash hair

To Learn More

AT THE LIBRARY

Bellisario, Gina. *Clean Monster!: Fight Germs and Viruses*. Minneapolis, Minn.: Lerner Publications, 2021.

Huddleston, Emma. *Taking Care of Your Body*. Lake Elmo, Minn.: Focus Readers, 2021.

Murray, Julie. *Staying Safe with Healthy Habits*. Minneapolis, Minn.: Abdo Publishing, 2021.

ON THE WEB

FACTSURFER

Factsurfer.com gives you a safe, fun way to find more information.

1. Go to www.factsurfer.com.

2. Enter "keeping clean" into the search box and click 🔍.

3. Select your book cover to see a list of related content.

Index

The images in this book are reproduced through the courtesy of: Anurak Pongpatimet, front cover (kid brushing teeth); yulya_talerenok, front cover (bathroom); IL21, p. 3; Nadasaki, pp. 4-5; JenJ Ivary, pp. 6-7; Africa Studio, pp. 8-9; Prasit Rodphan, pp. 10-11; Brothers91, p. 11 (stay healthy); Dean Mitchell, p. 11 (keeps germs away); ESB Professional, p. 11 (feel confident); PR Image Factory, pp. 12-13; StockPlanets, pp. 14-15; vgajic, pp. 16-17; nikkytok, p. 17 (shampoo); Yuganov Konstantin, p. 17 (soap); Lia Koltyrina, p. 17 (toothbrush, toothpaste, and floss); Wavebreak Media ltd/ Alamy, pp. 18-19; Elena Nichizhenova, pp. 20-21; TY Lim, p. 22 (confident); Serezniy, p. 22 (floss); vchal, p. 22 (germs); Dmytro Zinkevych, p. 22 (shampoo); Userba011d64_201, p. 23 (kid washing hands).